How to Advertise Your Hair Salon Business on Facebook and Twitter

ISBN-13: 978-1479298068
ISBN-10: 1479298069

Copyright Notice

HOW TO ADVERTISE YOUR HAIR SALON BUSINESS ON FACEBOOK AND TWITTER:

Mandy Winters

I dedicate this to anyone who's been touched by the joy, excitement and buzz of getting a new hairstyle...

Contents

- Ask Questions
- Run Contests
- Study Your Results
- Targeted Advertising
- Groups
- Your Facebook 'To Do' Checklist

Twitter

- Improve Your Hair Salon Business Sales With Twitter
- The 5 Benefits of Twitter Marketing for Your Hair Salon Business
- Establish Your Brand and Raise Awareness
- Pitch Products in a More Personal Way
- Draw Attention
- Conduct Market Research
- Strengthen Your Customer Service
- Why Use Twitter to Market Your Hair Salon Business?
- Studying the Competition
- What Your Profile Says About You
- Your Background Design
- Biography
- A Picture Is Worth...a Thousand Twitter Followers?
- Targeting Followers
- Getting Followers from Other Online Properties
- Talk Directly To People
- Personal Service

- Search... and You Shall Find
- Lists
- Managing Your Online Reputation
- Trends In The Hair Industry
- Get Chatting
- Essential Twitter Business Tools

Why Use Social Media for Your Hair Salon?

Over 75% of online consumers use social media every day. So you can't afford to ignore using social media in your hair salon business.

Your goal when using social media is to become part of the community. This means you should never try to sell on social media.

Rather, focus on building your credibility and the trust of your potential hair salon customers.

The idea is to get people to like and trust you enough to click through to your website and then you can sell from there.

The 6 Benefits of Social Media Marketing for Your Hair Salon Business

Social media has been getting a lot of buzz these days. If you're still wondering why people are making such a big deal, then read on to find out what benefits social media has to offer your business.

1. **Establish Your Brand and Raise Awareness**

The vast majority of the population already use social media sites like Facebook and Twitter.

Therefore, placing your brand name on these networks will increase the chances of people knowing your hair salon business exists.

2. Spy on Your Competition

Follow your closest competitors on Facebook and Twitter, and see what deals they offer and what marketing strategies they use.

3. Pitch Products In a More Personal Way

Social media sites have a personal and casual feel, which means you can build a better connection with your target market by discussing business in a fun and casual way.

You can ask for their opinions and respond to their queries in real time, which is an excellent way of winning brand loyalty.

4. Draw Attention

One of the fastest ways to draw attention to a product is by featuring it on a social media site along with a special promotion for online community members.

5. Conduct Market Research

Take note of your customers' feedback and keep track of what links they click on. This will help you gauge what customers like and what type of ad they usually respond to. People love expressing their opinions on social media sites, so this is the perfect venue for you to hear the truth. You can then use the information you gather to make improvements in your products, services, or marketing strategies.

6. Strengthen Your Customer Service

Social media networks not only allow you to address customers' concerns in a more personal way, but also in a timelier manner. This will improve customer satisfaction.

Here's how you can take advantage of social media as an online marketing tool:

1. Start a Blog

Did you know that you can also use blogs to communicate directly with potential patrons of your business?

In fact, blogging has now become one of the most effective online marketing strategies. Because of its popularity many business owners have begun using their blog to drive traffic to their main websites.

You can even use your blog to convert your fellow bloggers into loyal customers.

There are several sites that allow you to maintain a blog for free. One of the easiest and most popular is Wordpress. Be sure to choose a blog name that is relevant to your website and is catchy and inviting.

When you start creating content for your blog, you should make sure, of course, that it is relevant to your business and your target audience.

You may include industry-specific tips, special offers, product reviews, tutorials, and competitions in your blog content.

You should also encourage your readers to post questions, comments, or feedback about the topics and the blog itself.

When they do post questions, comments, and feedback, be sure to respond to them promptly.

People generally like being noticed and personal attention to their questions and comments will make them appreciate and trust you more.

Keep your blog fresh by posting new content as often as possible (once a week is a good schedule).

Blogging has become one of the most popular ways for people to air their opinions on certain issues.

Write Informative Blog Posts

If you want to encourage people to visit your site, then make sure your blog posts are informative, substantial and interesting.

Comment on Other Blogs

Visit other blog sites and look for hot topics. When you find popular topics that are relevant to your niche, post comments and guide the other visitors to your own site.

As people begin to see you as an authority in the field, more people will visit your site more frequently.

With more regular visitors, not only will your web traffic increase, but your customers' lifetime value (LTV) will increase as well.

Post Comments and Answer Questions

When you're at a dinner party, you don't just sit around listening to other people's stories without making a single comment, right?

The same is true with social media.

You have to get involved in conversations in order to build your credibility and your reputation as an authority in your field. This will encourage more people to check out your blog and visit your website.

You may even want to link back to blog posts or articles that are relevant to a particular conversation.

The more involved you are in social media, the more you will be seen as a trusted expert.

Eventually, your good reputation will lead to higher conversion rates and bigger revenue.

Create a Forum on Your Site

People always appreciate being able to interact with other people in real time.

For this reason, creating a forum on your site where your existing customers and potential clients can interact with each other is definitely a good way of driving traffic to your site.

If you make the forum a permanent part of your site's features, then your visitors and clients can easily communicate with each other without leaving your site.

You can take note of their questions and comments, and use them to make improvements in your products and services.

Be Interactive

Aside from allowing your visitors to interact with each other, you have to make it a point to interact with them as well.

People appreciate business owners who personally connect with them by commenting on their posts and responding to their queries promptly.

When you respond, try to be as personal with your answers and comments as possible.

When your guests see that you value them individually, they will be more likely to stay loyal to you and your hair salon business.

2. Set-up Facebook, Twitter, and LinkedIn Accounts

These services are among the most popular social media sites and they're sure to give your hair salon business more exposure and allow you to reach out to more potential customers.

The best bit is they're all free and very easy to set up.

As soon as you have set-up your accounts, start posting links to your blog and to your website. If anyone asks about them, be sure to respond promptly.

You may also want to use a service like Hootsuite, which allows you to keep tabs on all of your social media accounts, monitor conversations, and schedule updates all in one venue.

Social Networks

Social networks have now become the lifeline of online interaction.

Sites like Facebook, Twitter and Linkedin are great ways to indirectly market your products and services to friends and followers.

With Twitter, advertising can be as easy as posting a one-liner message with a direct link to your website. This can be done during your breaks or at idle times throughout the day.

Just be careful not to spam on social networking sites and don't just tweet with links all the time.

Post some useful information without links from time to time just to build your credibility among your followers as well as other online community members.

Facebook

It's pretty hard to ignore Facebook. Facebook is the most popular website in the world.

Let me say that again.

Facebook is the most popular website in the world.

Second only to Google for number of site visitors per day, it's hugely popular throughout the world and an amazing source of traffic.
In this section we're going to cover the free and paid aspects of Facebook.

More than 500 million users are on Facebook. Over 50% of those users log into Facebook every day and the average user has 130 friends. People spend over 700 billion minutes per month on Facebook.

Facebook is the most popular website in the world and is second only to Google for site visitors per day
What you want to do is use Facebook to get traffic and intermix it into your hair salon business and remember your goal is to drive people to your own website to make sales.
For this reason, Facebook is one of the best ways to build your database of customers.

Free

A mistake a lot of people make when they first think about using Facebook for their business is they start building up their friends.

They accept friend request from people who they don't know and before they know it they end up with 3000 friends!

But if you think about it, it's not very smart. If the average person has 130 friends then you can imagine that 3000 is just too many to manage and there are all these people who you don't know.

If you're going to use Facebook for traffic and for hair salon business, I strongly urge you to create a page.

To create a page, look for the Facebook/pages link and follow the instructions, rather than use your personal account.

TIP: When you create your page have at least one other person with admin access in case you have any issues logging in at any time.

Marketing Your Hair Salon Business on Facebook

If you're not an active Facebook user, you might find it more than a bit confusing and you may not even have any idea how you can possibly turn Facebook posts into profit?

The good news is that it's so much easier than you may think, and this article will tell you all about it.

By simply looking at the numbers, you'll understand that ignoring Facebook as a marketing tool is no longer an option for business owners like you.

So, the only question that you need to ask at this point is:

"How can I use Facebook to my advantage?" Read on to find out.

Who's Using Facebook?

To start with, let's get one thing straight: Facebook is no longer just a social network for college kids.

It may have started out that way, but its millions of members are now almost equally divided across the entire demographic spectrum.

And perhaps the most visible proof that college kids no longer dominate the world of Facebook is the fact that the largest segment of users belong to the 35-54 age bracket, while the 55-and-above segment is considered as the fastest-growing.

Therefore, Facebook is most definitely an excellent way to reach your target market, regardless of who they are and what age bracket they belong to.

How to Market on Facebook

There are three tools you can use to market your hair salon business on Facebook.

Each of these tools has its own set of advantages and disadvantages, and you can even choose to combine all three for greater reach and optimum results.

Pages

These are similar to Facebook profiles, except for the fact that it's meant for public figures, businesses, and organizations.

Another difference is that a profile owner has to confirm your request so you can be added to his list of friends, but anyone can like a page and be connected to it without the creator having to accept any request.

And unlike profiles, pages don't have any restriction where the number of friends or fans is concerned.

The advantage of marketing your hair salon business on a Facebook page is that it's very easy to set-up and completely free of charge.

The disadvantage, however, is that it can be quite difficult to build a fan base.

Ads

Did you know that Facebook has a wonderful targeted advertising platform you can take advantage of?

With this tool, you can post advertisements and target it at specific age groups, geographic areas, or college majors, among other categories.

And the fact that Facebook users are free to click or close any advertisement that appears on their profile means that better-targeted advertisements are constantly being delivered.

The main advantage of this marketing tool is that has very powerful targeting parameters. But, the disadvantage is that it can be quite costly, depending on your advertising goals.

Groups

These are similar to discussion forums on other websites, but with added features that are similar to what profiles and pages have to offer.

It's a good idea to create a group related to the hair salon industry or products and services because it can be a great way to reach out to and interact with both your existing customers and potential customers.

The biggest advantage of this tool is that it promotes high engagement levels and just like pages, it's completely free.

The disadvantage is that it has a tendency to be extremely time-consuming.

Marketing with Pages

1. Create Landing Pages

The custom tabs you see on Facebook pages allow you to create different landing pages for different types of users.

For example, existing customers and page fans may be brought to a landing page that offers special discounts or promotions, while those who aren't fans yet could be brought to a landing page that offers valuable information on why it's a good idea for them to like your page.

The following companies have excellent Facebook landing pages:

Starbucks – their landing page contains a tab dedicated to their rewards card users.

Vitamin Water – their home tab provides you with product information along with reasons why you should like their page

These are all excellent examples of how you can use the custom tabs on your page to create unique landing pages.

You can use them for inspiration in marketing your own hair salon business venture.

2. Post Useful Information

Take note that everything you post on your wall will appear in the news feed of all your page fans. Therefore, you need to make sure that everything you post will be of use to them; otherwise, they might deem your page useless and un-like it.

Useful posts may include new product announcements, coupon codes offering savings on your products, links to industry- or company-related articles, and links to online tools you believe would be useful to your fans.

Aside from ensuring that all posts are useful, you should also avoid posting too many times each day unless you have a special game or event going on.

Remember that spamming is one of the fastest ways for you to lose your fans.

3. Ask Questions

People just love it when they're given a chance to become more involved in any business.

And because Facebook is primarily a social networking site, you're more likely to earn the loyalty of your fans if you get them involved. Ask questions related to your industry, your products, or your niche. And as much as possible, try to ask open-ended questions so as to encourage more discussion and garner the best responses.

Getting feedback in this manner also assures your customers that you truly care about their opinions and that you're truly committed to addressing their needs and wants.

4. Run Contests

Contests can work to your advantage in at least two ways: it can inspire loyalty from your existing fans and help you earn new fans.

Simply by offering a hundred dollars worth of prize and spending a few days setting up a contest, you could earn hundreds of new fans in exchange.

So, you now could have hundreds of potential customers who receive your updates each day.

5. Study Your Results

Aside from custom tabs, Facebook also offers great analytics you can use to keep track of your page results.

Take advantage of these tools. If you notice a significant change in your results – a sudden surge or reduction of fans – check your recent posts and try to figure out if there's a trend.

You may then post more of that type of content if it results in a surge of fans, or avoid it if it results in a drop-off.

Targeted Advertising

That fact that it has a wealth of demographic information about users makes Facebook one of the best tools for targeted online advertising.

You can choose to target potential customers based on just about any information on users' profiles.

What's best is that you can also track your advertising success for each targeted segment. Facebook allows you to run ads on a per-click or per-impression basis.

You'll also be able to view what the current bids are for similar ads, so you'll known if your bid is still in line with other industry players.

You also have the option of setting daily limits to make sure you don't go out of budget.

You can choose from several different types of ads, and you can opt to have the ads direct users to your Facebook page or to your own website.

You may also post ads promoting an event on your Facebook page and equip it with an RSVP link.

You may also create advertisements for your Facebook groups and applications.

And except for Facebook event advertisements, all ads you run on Facebook will be equipped with a "Like" button.

The effectiveness of your advertisement increases with each click on this button.

And in the case of ads for your Facebook page, liking the ad also automatically makes a person a fan of your page.

And even if a user closes your ad, it still isn't a complete loss because users are typically asked why they decided to close an ad, and you can use this information to improve on future ads.

As previously mentioned, Facebook allows you to target your advertising campaigns based on just about anything you can find on a user's profile.

For example, you may want to target by location, if you feel that's an important factor for your hair salon business.

After specifying the location, you can then move on to targeting by demographics, which can include interests, age, and relationship status, among others. The advertising potential is virtually limitless.

One huge advantage of targeted advertising is the fact that you can create a different ad for each demographic group.

If, for example, you're targeting hat fans, you can create a different ad for each popular hat type. Take note that better-targeted ads are more likely to earn better results.

Groups

Aside from a Facebook page, a group is also an excellent way of building a community around your hair salon business.

This is essentially a much less commercial tool than pages, but it can still serve a marketing purpose.

The biggest advantage of groups is that they promote discussion and participation much better than pages do in most cases.

The best way to take advantage of a Facebook group is to create one based not on your business, but on the industry or niche that you serve.

Now, how do you foster discussion in your group?

First of all, you'll need to set some clear policies regarding the content of posts and comments in your group.

Be sure to post these policies such that all group members will be sure to see them. You may then start a discussion and encourage members to start their own as well.

Remember as well that you'll need to moderate your discussion boards regularly to ensure you don't get overrun by spammers.

Take note that groups don't just allow you to foster discussions, but also to send out bulk messages to all members.

You can use this tool to send out weekly or monthly newsletters, or to highlight discussions which you feel your members will find interesting. Be careful not to send too many bulk messages, though.

And make sure you only send important content. Group members are likely to get upset and leave your group if you send messages too often or if you send too many unimportant messages.

One disadvantage of creating and managing a Facebook group is that it can be extremely time-consuming, especially where moderating discussion boards is concerned.

One alternative you may want to consider is joining groups that are closely related to your own industry or niche.

This is an excellent way of building awareness for your hair salon business, but you'll have to be very careful in promoting your hair salon business to other group members because there are groups that have very strict policies.

The moment they see you posting commercial content, they're likely to ban you from the group, thus causing you to lose goodwill.

Therefore, you'll need to check group policies beforehand and adhere to it in order to build goodwill.

So, now you understand that Facebook isn't just capable of becoming a powerful marketing tool, but it can also be a very flexible tool.

Regardless of what type of business you have, you'll surely find a marketing option that fits your budget and suits your hair salon business.

Sure, it can take a while to learn all of its features, but the time spent is certainly worth the rewards you can get.

Facebook continues to grow each day, so it's definitely a good idea to take advantage of it.

If Facebook still isn't a part of your hair salon business marketing campaign, then it should be. Tinker around and launch a few test campaigns until you get the hang of it.

As with anything else, practice makes perfect, and the best time to start practicing is now!

Your Facebook 'To Do' Checklist

☐ 1. Set up a Facebook account.

☐ 2. Set up a separate "page" and post articles and information here.

☐ 3. Add coupons, special offers and links to your Facebook page to drive people to your site.

☐ 4. Make sure to include a clickable link http://www.yoursite.com on your page which leads visitors back to your site.

☐ 5. Commit to putting time into posting on Facebook every week.

Twitter

Marketing Your Hair Salon Business on Twitter

Twitter may not be quite as popular as Facebook, but it does have a number of advantages.

For one thing, it's much easier to gain Twitter followers than Facebook page fans.

It's also possible to interact with people on Twitter even before they become your friends or fans.

This section provides you with a guide on how to set-up your Twitter profile and launch a successful marketing campaign on the site.

This section is especially useful for those who are new to Twitter as well as people looking for some fresh marketing ideas.

Studying the Competition

It's always a good idea to check out what your competitors are doing so you'll have an idea of what works and what doesn't.

Checking out the competition is also a good way for you to determine how you can set yourself apart.

You can find the Twitter accounts of your competitors by checking their website or using online directories like Wefollow and Twefollow, which allows you to search for Twitter users according to the industry where they belong.

Take inspiration from a similar business that has a large Twitter following.

What Your Profile Says About You

Before you even start looking for Twitter followers, you'll have to make sure you have a good profile first.

After all, your profile is the first thing people see of your account, so it has to be interesting enough to draw potential followers.

The most essential elements you need to include in your profile are the following:

1. Your Background Design

Someone who views your profile for the first time should see an interesting background that perfectly reflects your brand or the image you want your hair salon business to project.

2. Biography

Twitter allows you to use a total of 160 characters to tell people who you are and what you have to offer, so make the most of it.

To make sure your bio is interesting enough to earn followers, write down and edit it a number of times before actually posting it to your profile. You may even want to consider getting feedback from family and friends beforehand.

3. A Picture Is Worth... a Thousand Twitter Followers?

People are hardly likely to follow you if your profile contains a generic Twitter icon. Likewise, not many people are convinced to follow a logo, unless it's a very popular logo.

You'll have a better chance of getting followers if you include a profile picture.

After all, is primarily about interaction, and people naturally want to interact with other people, rather than bots or impersonal establishments.

4. Excellent Tweets

Take note that people usually make the final decision on whether to follow someone or not based on their most recent tweets.

Therefore, you should make sure your tweets are interesting and that they reflect your level of engagement with your audience.

Your tweets should provide useful information and respond to other tweets more than they try to deliver a sales pitch.

Targeting Followers

As soon as your profile is properly set-up and you have started posting some interesting tweets, it's time to gain followers.

And while you can get just about anyone to follow you, it's best to target followers who are actually interested in your industry or niche.

The question is:

How do you find these individuals and get them to follow you?

While not everything is about numbers, it still works to your advantage to have someone visit your profile and see that you have a great follower count.

A good strategy would be to look for people who have put in place a follow-back policy, which means that when you follow them, an application will automatically let them follow you as well.

Start following people who work in the same or similar industry and take advantage of the follow-back policy to build your own initial set of followers as well.

As much as possible, look for people whose ratio of followers and following count is 1:1 or as close to that as possible.

TwitterCounter Search and Twitter lists in Listorious are great places for you to conduct your search.

By entering your password in TwitterCounter Search, you'll be able to view users as well as their follower and following count. Simply connect your TwitterCounter with your account, and you can start following users directly from their results.

With Listorious, you'll be able to view lists compiled by other Twitter users belonging to your industry.

You'll see the profiles along with follower and following count on the right side of your Twitter screen, and you'll also have the option to follow them directly.

Other than these two methods, you can also build a follower base by using Wefollow and Twefollow as mentioned above.

There are also several applications you can take advantage of, which automate the Twitter following process.

The most popular of these applications is Tweet Adder, which helps you find and follow new users based on your customized searches.
It also un-follows users who don't follow you back within a specific period.

Getting Followers from Other Sites

Do you have an existing website, blog, or any other online property?

If so, then you should be sure to include your Twitter link in all of your online posts, including your forum signature, e-mail signature, and other social media profiles.

This will make it easier for people who are already connected with you to find and follow you on Twitter.

If you have a blog, then you'd do well to use the "retweet" button to allow your blog visitors to share your blog posts to their Twitter friends.

The best news is that adding this button to your blog also allows you to share your Twitter account, thus automatically inviting people who are already interested in your industry to follow you.

Talk Directly To People

So, you already have plenty of followers.
That's good news indeed, but it's no reason for you to relax just yet.

The most important step is yet to come, and that is interacting with your followers.

One very effective way to establish a connection is through direct messages.

Take note, though, that Twitter users typically have a love/hate relationship with direct messages because of the proliferation of spam.

The more you follow other users, the more you'll see examples of both good and bad messages. As much as possible, you should avoid pitching your products and services at the outset or trying to get your followers to opt-in to your mailing list.

You should think of your first direct message as the very first thing you say to someone you've just met.

You wouldn't want to put them off by immediately going into a sales pitch, right?

What you need to do instead is simply thank them for following you and then ask them what they'd like to learn from you.

Their response to the latter will help you determine what kinds of tweets are likely to keep them interested in your hair salon business.

Of course, the best way to send out direct messages is to personalize them.

But, as your followers grow in number, it can be quite impractical to keep doing this, and this is where automation starts to play a major role.

There are several free services like SocialOomph that allow you to register your Twitter account and send direct messages automatically.

Remember, though, that you should always try to reply personally to followers who respond to your messages.

It's also a good idea to keep track of who sends direct messages to you as well.

For example, if there are people who send messages asking you to help promote their blog content, you should take note of who they are.

The next time you have something that you really need to push, send them direct messages as well; it's your turn to ask for a favour.

Personal Service

The term "automation" is often seen in a negative light in the world of social media primarily because the realization that an account is actually nothing more than an automated bot can be the biggest turn-off for a social media user.

The most important and beneficial Twitter updates are still those that you post personally and where you're able to interact directly with your followers as well as the major players in your industry.

Replying regularly with an @username is the key to assuring your followers that you're not just an automated bot, but an actual human being who's willing to communicate directly with them.

Search... And You Shall Find

Twitter searches allow you to monitor all tweets that include a particular keyword.

For example, you could set-up a Twitter search in an application like HootSuite and assign a keyword.

You'll then be able to see all tweets associated with this keyword.

If a customer asks a question as to where she can get the best conditioner for frizzy hair, you can immediately @username reply to her and share a link to your website where she can find the answer to her question.

Another option would be to make use of Twitter's advanced search tool to get even more detailed searches.

Lists

These lists allow you to add up to 500 people to specific lists so you can monitor activity on their accounts.

This is an excellent way for you to identify thought leaders in your industry or niche.

It's easy enough to create lists and add users to it, and by following the users on your lists, you'll learn what particular topics are the most important in your industry, re-tweet posts about these topics, and respond to your followers if they have questions about these topics.

Twitter lists can also help you categorize your followers according to location, keywords on their bio, or other factors.

You can even use these lists to cross-reference people whom your followers interact with that you may also want to connect with.

Managing Your Online Reputation

Another great strategy for building your reputation online is by monitoring any mention of your hair salon business, brand, products, blog, or website by creating keyword searches on HootSuite for those keywords.

This will make it easy for you to identify and thank everyone who has good words for your hair salon business, and respond promptly to anyone who may have some issues or negative commentary.

Dealing with issues on a public platform is also a good way of showing existing and potential customers alike that your top priority is their satisfaction.

And this is likely to lead to more positive sentiments towards you and your business.

Trends In The Hair Industry

Another way to spread a message to people other than your own followers is to attach it to a currently popular topic or hashtag (#keyword).

The ten most popular hashtags are typically listed on the right side of your home page.

You have the option of changing your settings to reflect worldwide trends or industry-specific trends.

Any message you attach to a hashtag will be seen by all users following that particular topic.

The only drawback to this strategy is that it may not really apply to every single industry.

Get Chatting

Finally, you can participate in relevant Twitter chats to get more involved with your Twitter community.

Joining relevant chats often leads to an increase in the number of followers as well as a surge in website traffic, in case you have web content that's directly associated with the current topic of the chat.

By now, you should have at least a general idea on how you can take advantage of Twitter both for interacting with your online community and for marketing your hair salon business online.

You can tinker with the various features of this social medium and use the more advanced tools as you become more adept at using Twitter as an online marketing tool.

Your 'To Do' Twitter Checklist

☐ 1. Set up a Twitter account.

☐ 2. Tweet daily.

☐ 3. Tweet out coupons, sale information and links to your website to drive people to your site.

☐ 4. Always include a clickable link http://www.yoursite.com on your profile which leads visitors back to your site.

Essential Twitter Business Tools

Mainstream business has now recognized Twitter as a great tool not only for communication, but also for a host of other functions.

Here's a list of the most useful Twitter tools you can utilize in your hair salon business:

Analytics

These are the tools that'll help you determine how popular or influential your business is on Twitter:

1. TweetStats – An application offering a graphical analysis of your Twitter statistics.

2. Twinfluence – An application that measures Twitter influence according to velocity, reach, and social capital.

3. Twitter Grader – An application that informs you of your current Twitter grade and your local Twitter Elite. It also helps you find new users to follow.

4. Tweet-Rank – An application that lets you know which of your tweets made you earn or lose followers.

5. Retweetrank – An application that informs you of the number of retweets you and other users have.

6. Twitterholic – An application that shows you who the top users are and what your current Twitter statistics are.

7. Twitter Friends – An application allowing you to measure your conversations carefully on Twitter.

8. Tweetwasters – An application showing you how much time you and others regularly spend on Twitter.

9. Mr. Milestone – An application that tweets you each time you reach a Twitter milestone.

Market Research

These are the tools you can use for market research, to check out the competition, for your blog posts, and even for information-gathering purposes:

1. Twitterverse – An application that allows you to check archived tweets and timelines.

2. TwitterBuzz – An application that tells you what posts are being linked to by the most number of users on Twitter.

3. Tweetscan – An application that alerts you to any reply to your tweets or search queries.

4. TweetNews – An application that ranks posts according to the number of related tweets.

5. Retweetist – An application that ranks links
6. according to the number of retweets.

7. Twitscoop – An application that shares what's currently hot on Twitter.

8. Twitbuzz – An application that helps you track popular links and the latest Twitter conversations.

9. StrawPoll – An application that enables you to share your opinions as easily as sending @ replies.

10. Monitter – An application allowing for real-time monitoring of keywords on Twitter.

11. @myflightinfo – An application that provides you with updates on your flight status.

It also allows you to chat with other Twitter users who are interested in the same topics.

Social Networking

These are the applications that'll help you find users who may be interested in your products and services:

1. Twitter Local – An application that allows you to view tweets from users in specific locations.

2. Tweepler – An application allowing you to organize tweeps according to whether you're following them or not.

3. Just Tweet It – An application that helps you find Twitter bots, Tweeple, and other useful tools for your business.

4. TweetWheel – An application that helps you identify Twitter friends who know each other.

5. Mr. Tweet – An application that helps you find relevant followers, thus serving as an excellent personal networking assistant.

6. Nearbytweets – An application that provides you with information about all Twitter users in a particular area.

7. Twitoria – An application that helps reduce clutter on your Twitter account by identifying connections who haven't tweeted in quite a while.

8. TwitDir – An application that allows you to search for people and explore user categories like top updaters and top followers.

9. Twellow – An application that helps you find Twitter users in specific industries.

10. Qwitter – An application that alerts you every time a user stops following you.

11. Twubble – An application that identifies people you may want to follow.

12. SocialToo – An application that helps you keep track of all users who have followed or stopped following you.

13. Who Should I Follow? – An application that provides you with recommendations on ideal tweeps to follow.

14. Follow Cost – An application that informs you of the amount of effort needed to follow a particular user.

15. MyCleenr – An application that helps you sort your connections according to their last tweets. It helps you get rid of inactive and useless accounts.

Managing Your Account

These are the applications you can use to build your Twitter following fast:

1. Twitterless – An application that notifies you whenever someone stops following you on Twitter.

2. TwitterSnooze – An application that pauses a particular user for a specified amount of time.

3. TweepSearch – An application that allows you to search for followers according to specific parameters.

4. Tweetdeck – An application that provides you with a more efficient manner of keeping track of users you truly want to be updated about.

5. Tweet O'Clock – An application that informs you of the best time to get someone's attention.

6. TwitResponse – An application that allows you to schedule the posting of tweets ahead of time.

7. Twilert – An application that alerts you every time a specific keyword is used on Twitter.

8. Twalala – An application that allows you to stop the tweets of certain users or about specific topics, in case you've been getting a lot of updates you don't really find interesting.

9. Friend or Follow – An application that lets you know which among the users you follow do not follow you back and vice versa.

10. Just Signal – An application that allows you to set-up filters that limit the tweets you get to those that discuss keywords you're most interested in.

11. Summize – An application that allows you to quickly retrieve information on Twitter and conduct real-time searches on the site.

Tweet-sharing

These are the applications you can use to share photos and promote your business, among other things:

1. TwitterHawk – An application that provides you with targeted marketing options on Twitter.

2. Tweetburner – An application allowing you to share links and track their usage.

3. TweeTube – An application allowing you to share videos easily on Twitter.

4. Twitpic – An application that allows you to take and share mobile phone photos easily using your Twitter account.

5. Twisten.fm – An application that allows you to share what you're currently listening to on Twitter.

6. Twiggit – An application that allows you to share articles that you dig on Twitter.

7. Acamin – An application allowing you to share files easily with your Twitter followers.

8. Glue – An application allowing you to posts links to restaurants, books, and movies, among other things.

9. Ping.fm – An application that's capable of simultaneously updating all of your social network accounts.

Getting Organized

These are the applications you can use to automate your Twitter tasks:

1. Twittercal – An application allowing you to link your Twitter to Google Calendar so you can easily manage events and appointments.

2. TwitterNotes – An application allowing you to organize your notes on Twitter.

3. Tweetake – An application that provides a backup for your Twitter timeline for archiving purposes.

4. Tweet Later – An application allowing you to schedule tweets, send direct messages, and set-up alerts easily.

5. OutTwit – An application allowing you to use Twitter inside Outlook.

6. TrackThis – An application that tweets you every time there's a location change for just about anything you want to track.

7. Joint Contact – An application that provides you with great project management productivity.

8. Timer – An application that reminds you of current tasks through Twitter.

9. Jott – An application that allows you to transcribe voice messages to Twitter.

10. Tempo – An application allowing you to send updates from Twitter.

11. Toodledo – A to-do list application that can easily be integrated with Twitter.

12. Nozbe – An application allowing you to add to or update your to-do list easily on Twitter.

13. Remember the Milk – An application that allows you to update your to-do list.

Managing Your Life

These are the applications that help you build relationships and manage your daily affairs:

1. 21Tweets – An application that offers personal coaching via Twitter.

2. Tweet Answers – An application allowing you to ask questions and get answers easily on Twitter.

3. Vacatweet – An application that allows you to set-up an auto-responder for your account.

4. ConnectTweet – An application that allows you to put together the voices of all members of your group.

5. Tweeteorology – An application that informs you about the weather in a location of your choice.

6. DreamTweet – An application that allows you to track your dreams and nightmares as well as those of other users.

7. TwtTRIP – An application that lets you organize your travel plans and identify other travellers going your way.

8. Twtvite – An application that serves as an event organizer, which you can use to schedule tweetups.

9. TrackDailyGoals – An application that lets you keep track of your daily goals.

10. MyMileMarker – An application that allows you to keep track of your mileage.

11. plusplusbot – An application that allows you to share your feelings to other users.

Money Matters

These are the applications you can use to manage your finances via Twitter:

1. Twittertise – An application especially designed for advertising purposes, allowing you to schedule tweets and track click-throughs.

2. CheapTweet – An application that allows you to get all coupons and deals currently being discussed on Twitter.

3. Tweet What You Spend – An application that helps you effectively track your cash.

4. SalesTwit – An application that helps you get contact management for your Twitter account.

5. StockTwits – An application that sends real-time information on investment discussions currently going on in Twitter.

6. TwtQpon – An application allowing you to create Twitter coupons for your business.

7. Xpenser – An application that records your expenses for you.

8. Chipin – An application that lets you set a goal for a fund-raising campaign and allows your supporters to keep track of the campaign's progress.

9. Tipjoy – An application that works in a similar manner to Chipin, it also offers social payment methods for your cause.

Blogging

These are the applications you can use to link your blog to your Twitter account:

1. MyTwitter – An application that allows you to show your Twitter status on WordPress.

2. TwitterCounter – An application that allows you to display how many Twitter followers you currently have.

3. TwitterFeed – An application that allows you to promote your blog with a customized message on Twitter.

4. TwitThis – An application that allows you to send Twitter messages promoting your blog.

5. Twitpress – An application that sends out tweets each time you post a new entry on your blog.

6. FriendFeed – An application allowing you to announce your blog on Twitter.

Made in the USA
Middletown, DE
11 December 2017